Love and Licks.
RICKEY

Ann H. Lacey

Dr. ŖICKEY
Wednesday's Promise

Co Authors:
Ann H. Lacey &
Barbara Wunder Pratt

Illustrated by:
Michael Sparling

Layout and Design:
Tanya P. Lacey

Printed by:
St. Vincent Press

Dr. RICKEY "prescribes"
this book for children
ages 5 to 105.

Questions should be addressed to:
    Dr. RICKEY
    P.O. Box 239
    Spencerport, New York 14559

ISBN 0-9658395-0-8

Summary: A dog named RICKEY makes weekly visits to a local nursing home to bring happiness and friendship to the residents and staff.

Printed in Rochester, New York.

Foreword

A special dog visits Wedgewood Nursing Home every week. His name is RICKEY. RICKEY has perky ears, a cute face with a nice snout, and long fluffy fur that everyone would love to cuddle and hide their fingers in. His breed is Shetland Sheepdog, commonly known as Sheltie.

The nursing home that RICKEY visits is a home to many people, usually older adults, who need help to live in a healthy way. The adults are referred to as "residents" because they live, or reside, at the home. The residents may need help to take a bath, eat their meals, walk, or take their medicine.

Most of the residents at the nursing home have had a dog or cat at some time in their lives. They miss feeding, petting, and caring for their animals. When RICKEY comes to visit on Wednesdays, they smile wider and longer than any other time during the week. Some people save a bit of food from breakfast to give RICKEY as a treat. Others may say "Oh good, RICKEY is coming today! It must be Wednesday."

RICKEY brings smiles...and smiles are great!

Debbie Weller-Plucknette
Social Worker/Wedgewood Nursing Home

Special thanks to...

my husband, Bob, whose love and support
helped to make this book possible.

Barbara Pratt and Michael Sparling for their
creative contributions.

the residents and staff of Wedgewood Nursing
Home for their total support.

Ann H. Lacey

Ann H. Lacey

Thphis book is dedicated to my grandmother,
Anna R. Howard(1891-1984) and our first
Sheltie, A.J.(1982-1991). Nana's love for A.J.
inspired me to seek other nursing homes
where A.J.'s visits would be welcomed.

Ann H. Lacey

Dr. RICKEY is not an M.D.

Nor is he a Ph.D.

Dr. RICKEY has no real degree.

What he has is his pedigree.

You see, Dr. RICKEY is a D-O-G

Whose job in life is pet therapy.

"What is pet therapy?" you might ask.

It's a very simple, considerate task.

It's when people are given the opportunity

To visit with animals they seldom see.

To be certified in pet therapy, RICKEY did his best,

To complete and pass a special therapy test.

He then was examined by Dr. Lann, his vet

To make certain that he was a healthy pet.

With the story that follows, you will see

Just how important an animal can be

To people who can no longer care for a pet.

With a visit from RICKEY this need is now met.

Dr. RICKEY has four legs and a tail.

He walks on his rounds leaving smiles in his trail.

He doesn't use medicine or needles that stick.

He does all his curing with his paws and his lick.

His job as a "therapist" is to make people smile,

To make them feel good, if just for awhile.

He can't solve their problems or cure all their ills.

He brings comfort with love instead of with pills.

He goes on his visits to nursing homes daily,

Prancing among the residents gaily.

If someone won't talk or sits like a grump,

Dr. RICKEY soon brings them out of their slump.

He doesn't ask favors or make odd demands.

He wants only pats from their gentle hands.

An occasional treat surely cheers up his day.

He'll earn it with a trick, then he's on his way.

RICKEY'S assistant and chauffeur is Ann.

She takes him to visit in her dark green van.

They follow their schedule each day of the week.

The residents all know it's a promise they keep.

His visit to one home is always the same.

As he enters the door, they call out his name.

"It must be Wednesday," is their common cheer.

Both residents and staff are happy he's here.

Gladys in her wheelchair at the end of the hall

Wants more than a handshake from RICKEY'S left paw.

Her lap is just waiting for the Sheltie to sit.

She'd rather hug RICKEY than crochet or knit.

She once had a dog she fondly remembers.

And RICKEY, she finds, can relight those embers.

His smooth silky coat and sweet doggie smell

Bring back her dog, Lady, she remembers so well.

8

Now on to Jean and Marion, too.

These ladies have tricks they want him to do.

He sits and says "please" with a delicate bark.

It's his special lingo with his special spark.

John won't see RICKEY. He's having a bad day.

This sometimes happens, though it's sad to say.

Not everyone wants a visit from RICKEY.

We all have bad times. Some days are just icky.

H e then visits Harry a minute or so.

Harry looks down at him and chuckles real low.

He gives him a treat and a "Well, well, well."

Harry wants RICKEY to sit for a spell.

Then on to Mary who ruffles his fur.

She remembers her Scottie dog, so dear to her.

And Doris will smile and pat his head,

While Norma and Carl keep RICKEY well fed.

13

Joe calls him "Baby" and gives him a pat.

Now what should a dog say back to that?

George is resting, but opens his eyes.

To see RICKEY there is a welcome surprise.

Velma strokes his back. She smiles, then she sighs.

Irene doesn't speak, but follows him with her eyes.

He touches each resident in a different way.

Most will admit he makes their day.

14

All of a sudden, to RICKEY'S surprise,

Coming towards him is John with a gleam in his eyes.

He's decided that RICKEY might brighten his day.

It's the thing RICKEY does in his own special way.

With a whistle he calls for RICKEY to come near.

He reaches down slowly to scratch the dog's ear.

John soon forgets that his day was so bad.

With RICKEY he remembers the good times he's had.

Just a few more stops and his job will be done.

The residents all say that the time has been fun.

His visit is an important part of their day.

RICKEY'S their friend. What more can you say?

Now a check to make sure no one was missed.

The staff helps by looking at the resident list.

As usual RICKEY has completed his task.

He's shared love with everyone. That's all that they ask.

His visit is over. Now it's time to go.

As he heads for the door, his pace is quite slow.

He knows they will miss him, but he won't dismay.

It's only a week 'til he hears, "It's Wednesday!"

SpARLiNG ©'97

About the authors:

Ann H. Lacey lives with her husband, Bob, and their Sheltie, RICKEY, in Spencerport, N.Y. She has her Bachelor's degree in Education and a Master's degree in Reading. Ann takes RICKEY on regular pet therapy visits to local nursing homes, adult homes, hospitals, a children's group home, and the Ronald McDonald House of Rochester, N.Y.

Barbara Wunder Pratt is a free-lance writer who lives in Spencerport, N.Y. with her husband, Ken, and their four children. She has a B.S. degree in Education from S.U.N.Y. Geneseo and one in Journalism from S.U.N.Y. Brockport. She has written three other children's books and is a contributing writer for the *Suburban News*.

About the illustrator:

Our illustrator for the Dr. RICKEY series, Michael Sparling, lives in the Genesee Valley town of Perry, N.Y. with his wife, Abby. They share an art studio producing various types of art including portraits of loved ones, pet portraits, murals, and faerie houses. Michael "hopes everyone who picks up this book enjoys the goodness that has come from the Lacey's efforts, the warmth and patience of RICKEY with these gentle folk, and Barbara's creative effort in co-authoring the text." Inquiries about portrait work may be sent to Michael at Sparling Studios, P.O. Box 144, Perry, New York, 14530.